50 TRICKS WITH A DUNCAN® YO-YO®

Scholastic Publications Ltd.,
10 Earlham Street, London WC2H 9LN, UK

Scholastic Inc.,
730 Broadway, New York, NY 10003, USA

Scholastic Tab Publications Ltd.,
123 Newkirk Road, Richmond Hill,
Ontario L4C 3G5, Canada

Ashton Scholastic Pty. Ltd.,
PO Box 579, Gosford, New South Wales,
Australia

Ashton Scholastic Ltd.,
165 Marua Road, Panmure, Auckland 6,
New Zealand

First published by Scholastic Publications Limited,
1986

Designed and produced by
AUTUMN PUBLISHING LIMITED
10 Eastgate Square,
Chichester, West Sussex PO19 1JH

Illustrations by Pam Lander
Cover photograph by Colour Precision Studio,
Chichester

ISBN 0 590 70674 8

Printed in Great Britain by Hazell Watson & Viney Limited,
Member of the BPCC Group, Aylesbury, Bucks

50 TRICKS with a DUNCAN® YO-YO®

By Don Robertson
European Yo-Yo Champion

A Hippo Book
from Scholastic

Contents

Introduction

The secret of success with your Duncan Yo-Yo is simple. It is not a trick, but all a matter of concentration, practice and a little skill.

The important thing to learn is to throw a 'Spinner' (Trick No. 10, page 18). This throw forms the basis of the majority of tricks. Practise throwing a 'Spinner' until you are perfect.

Good luck, have fun! Practise hard and you too could become a champion!

Don Robertson

FIRST STEPS

HOW TO PREPARE THE DUNCAN YO-YO

When you buy your Duncan Yo-Yo you will find that, in most cases, the string has been looped twice around the axle. Leave it like this until you have mastered the trick of making the Yo-Yo run up and down the string. When you can do this with ease, take the Yo-Yo and untwist the string until you can slip a loop off the Yo-Yo. Allow the string to retwist itself. The Yo-Yo will now be able to spin freely at the end of the string, and you can attempt the other tricks in this book.

REPLACING A STRING

1 Remove old string with a sharp knife, like a penknife, making sure that you do not scratch the axle.

2 Untwist the new string until you have a loop that you can slip onto the Yo-Yo.

3 Allow the string to rewind itself.

4 Hold the Yo-Yo so that it hangs just above your feet. Cut the string approximately 10cms above your waist. The string will now be the right length.

5 Tie a loop on the end of the string and form a slip knot by drawing part of the string through the loop.

1 YO-YO CONTROL (Up and Down)

1 Put the slip knot on the middle finger of your right hand, just behind the first joint. (NB: If you are left-handed please mentally alter all instructions from 'right' hand to 'left' hand.) The slip-knot should be on the under side of your finger. The string should always run from your finger down the outer edge of the Yo-Yo.

2 Now, with the palm facing down, release the Yo-Yo. It will spin to the bottom of the string. As it reaches this point, smoothly raise the hand a little, and the Yo-Yo will climb back up the string. There is no need to jerk the string. You can either catch the Yo-Yo as it returns, or let it fall again.

This is the first trick that you will be asked to accomplish if you enter a competition.

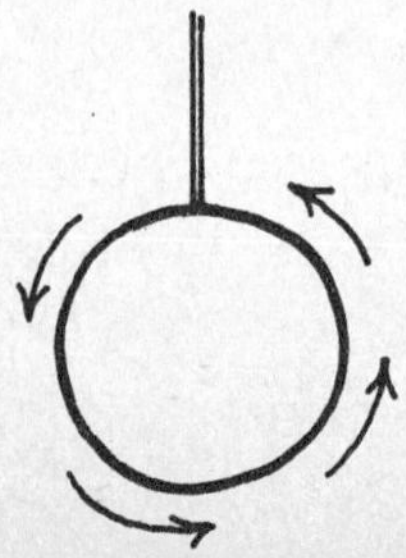

WINDING YOUR YO-YO

Most beginners start by holding the Yo-Yo in one hand and winding the string around the axle with the other hand. This is perfectly acceptable providing you make sure that the first two or three passes of the string around the axle are very loose. Eventually the string will 'catch', and you can then wind the Yo-Yo as normal. If you don't make the first two or three winds very loose, the Yo-Yo string will eventually become either very tight, so that the Yo-Yo cannot 'spin' freely at the end of the string; or so loose that it will not rise up the string.

TRICK METHODS OF WINDING THE YO-YO

2 FLOOR ROLL

Put the Yo-Yo on the floor, with most of the string lying on the ground. Give a sharp tug on the string. The Yo-Yo will roll along the ground winding itself up.

3 FLICK SPIN

1 Grasp the Yo-Yo with the left hand between thumb and index finger, with the string drawn over the right hand thumb.

2 Increase the tension on the string. Snap spin the Yo-Yo away from you with the thumb of your left hand.

3 A slight up and down motion of the right hand will bring the Yo-Yo back up into your hand, fully wound up.

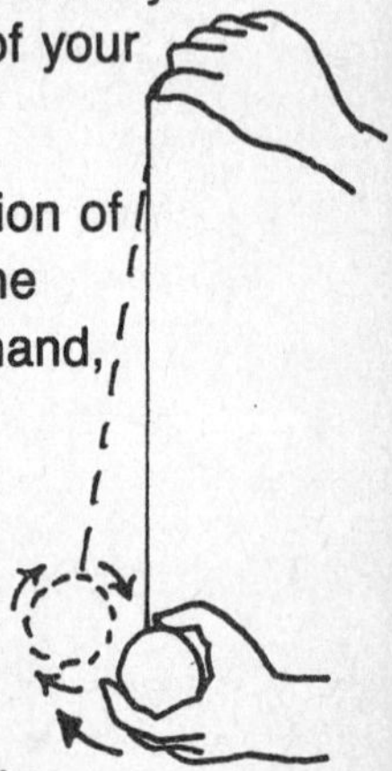

4 ONE HANDED WIND

1 Hold the Yo-Yo in your right hand, letting the string hang between the fingers (palm facing up).

2 A quick flick upwards and outwards will roll the Yo-Yo off the top of your fingers, making it spin rapidly. The first drop and pull up will return it to your hand.

5 HEEL AND PULLEY WIND

1 Place the Yo-Yo between heels, and loop string over top of left hand index finger.

2 Bend down so that left hand is about 40cms/16ins in front of the Yo-Yo, and several cms/ins above the ground.

3 Pull the string towards your body with the right hand. The Yo-Yo will roll out, and if the string is kept fairly slack, it should roll past the left hand, when a quick jerk will bring the Yo-Yo back to your right hand.

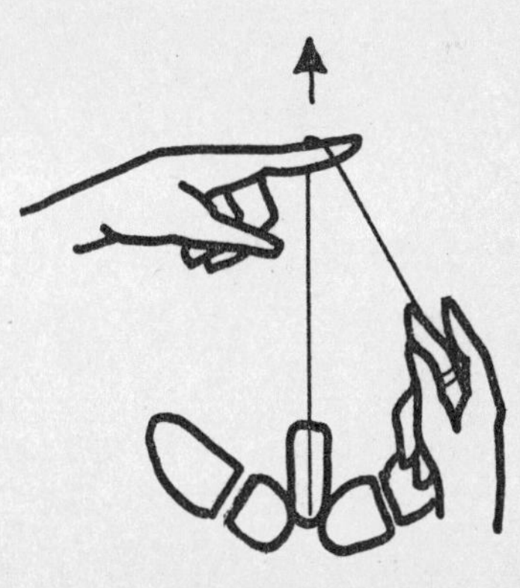

6 MONOROAIL WIND

1. Pass the string over the top of index finger of left hand (away from body). Bring the Yo-Yo to rest on the right hand, palm up. The Yo-Yo and the string on middle finger of right hand should be in a direct line.
2. Keep the left hand still. Raise right hand up in a semi-circle over the top of the left hand. The Yo-Yo will roll up its own string and over the left forefinger.
3. As it falls over left index finger drop your right hand with it, then with a smooth motion raise right hand, and the Yo-Yo will wind itself up to the top of the string.

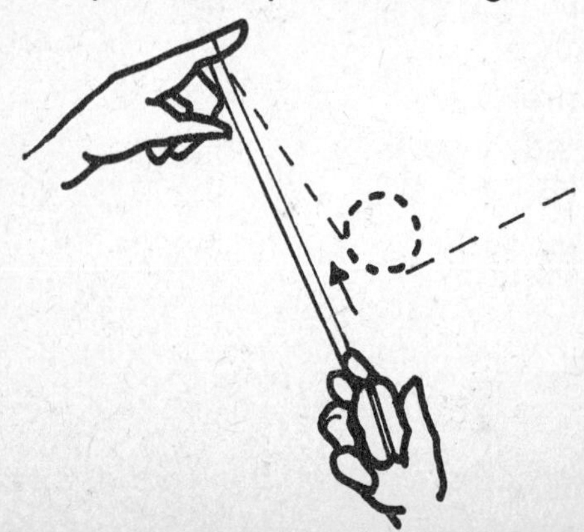

RETURNS

The ordinary return, as described in Yo-Yo control, is a simple catch by a hand, palm down, of the Yo-Yo on its return flight up the string.

Here are two trick returns.

7 PICK DROP RETURN

Once the Yo-Yo is in free 'spin' (see page 18) at the end of the string, take the string between thumb and index finger of the left hand, and lift it a few cms/ins. Then drop it suddenly. The Yo-Yo will climb rapidly up the string back into your hand.

8 THE KICK RETURN

Again, when the Yo-Yo is spinning freely at the bottom of the string, a quick tap with toe, or side of foot, will jerk the Yo-Yo, and the impetus will carry it back up the string.

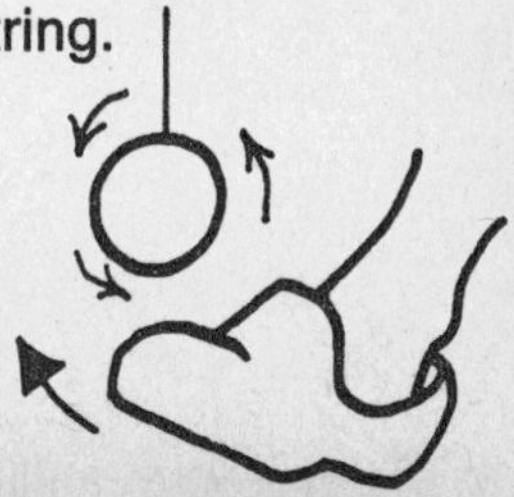

BASIC SIMPLE TRICKS

9 THE THROW, DOWN, OUT AND UP

1 The basic throw of the Yo-Yo is made by bending your arm at the elbow, with your hand facing your body, and the string over the top of the Yo-Yo.

2 The Yo-Yo is then thrown with a sharp downward fling of your hand, towards the ground.

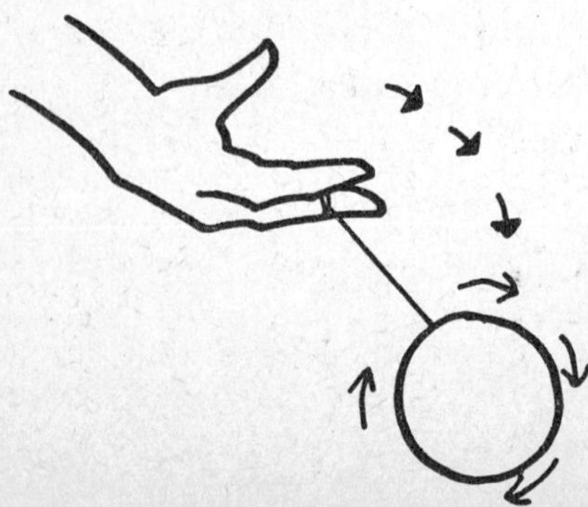

3 Turn your hand over so that the palm is facing down, and catch the Yo-Yo on its return flight up the string.

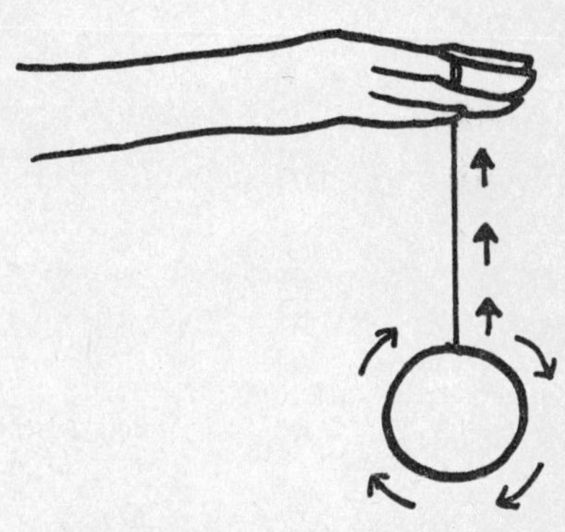

4 Two alternatives are:
OUT: throw the Yo-Yo sharply out in front, about waist high, and
UP: by flicking the wrist sharply back and then up, the Yo-Yo will go straight upwards.

10 THE SPINNER

1 Throw the Yo-Yo down (as described in the previous trick), but as soon as the Yo-Yo has left your hand, keep your hand and arm quite still.

2 The Yo-Yo will reach the bottom of the string where it will spin of its own accord.

3 Make sure that your palm is facing down and give the string a slight jerk. The Yo-Yo will climb back up the string into your hand.

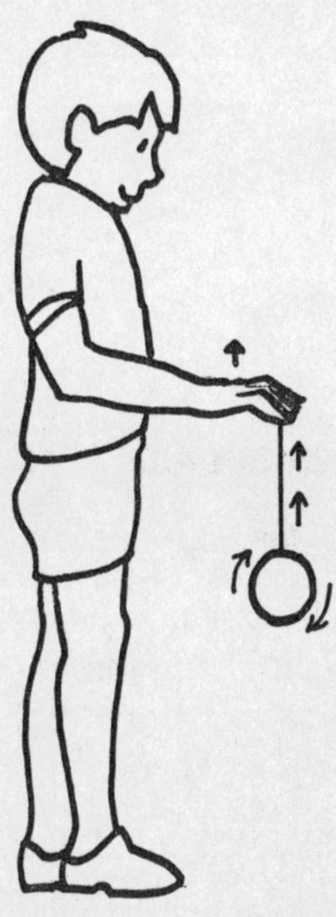

11 ARM AND KNEE JUMP

1 Throw a fast spinner, forwards and over outstretched left arm, so that Yo-Yo string is at a 90° angle.

2 Pause for a moment, then jerk string sharply and the Yo-Yo will leap up and over outstretched arm and back into your hand.

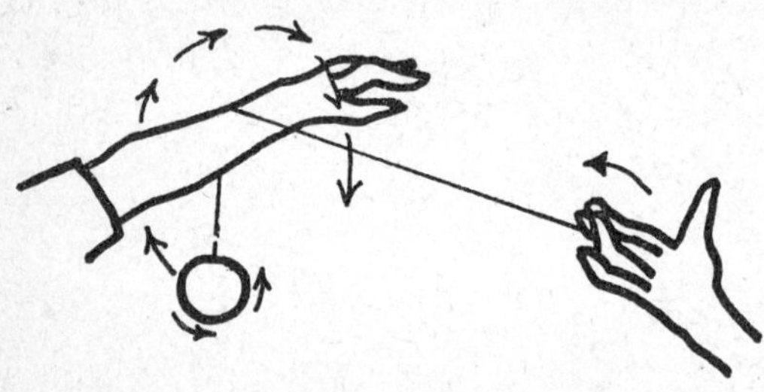

12 SPINNER SPLASH

1 Throw a fast spinner.

2 Catch the string with your left hand a few cms/ins from the Yo-Yo, and raise until string is at right-angles to your right hand.

3 Let go with left hand, flick wrist of right hand, and the Yo-Yo will go straight up in the air after circling close to the right hand. Catch the Yo-Yo.

13 MONKEY UP THE PALM

1 Throw a fast spinner, and hitch the string sideways over the tip of the middle finger.

2 Raise arm as high overhead as possible.

3 Allow the string hitched over middle finger to drop. This will flick the string. The Yo-Yo will shoot up the string and over the tips of the fingers and down again.

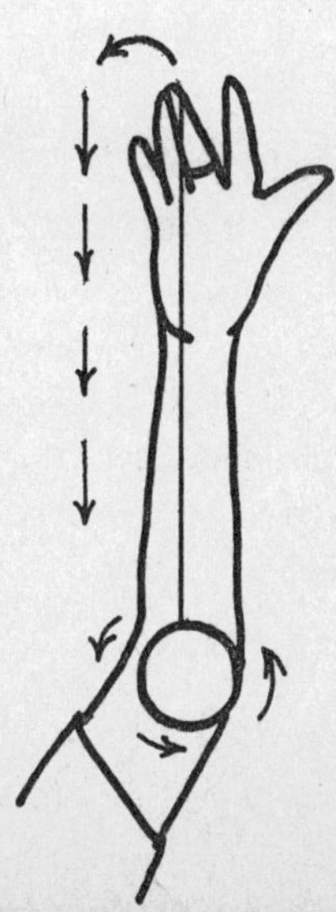

14 WALKING THE DOG

1 Throw a fast spinner (as described in the previous trick). Then gently lower your Duncan Yo-Yo to the floor.

2 Allow it to walk for a short distance in front of you.

3 Make sure there is no slack in the string until you are ready to return the Yo-Yo to your hand with a sharp upward flick of the wrist.

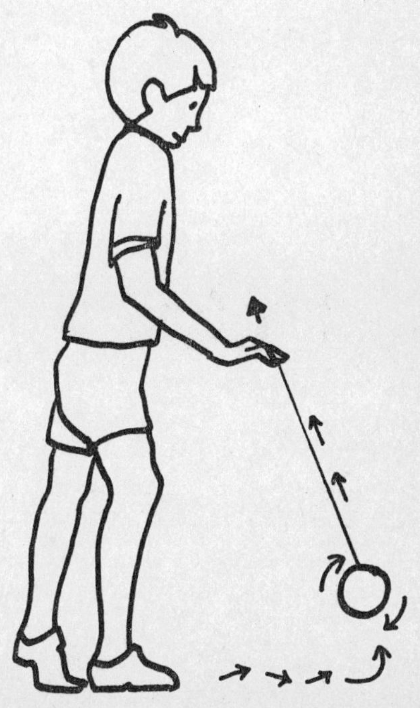

15 THE CREEPER

1 First throw a fast spinner.

2 Gently lower it to the floor and allow it to walk for a short distance (as in Walking the Dog), but bend your body so that your hand is just a few cms/ins off the ground.

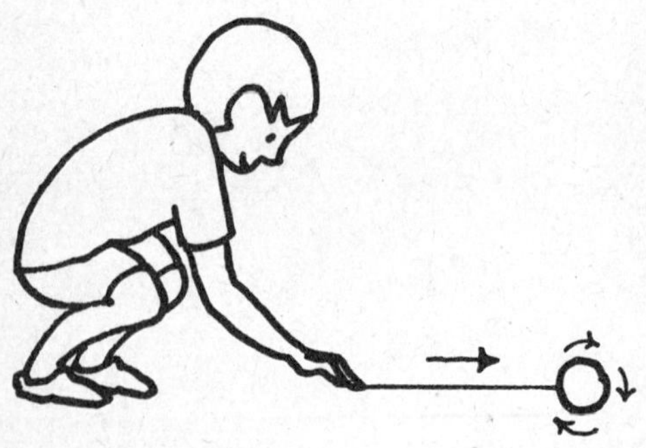

3 The Yo-Yo will crawl along the ground until it reaches the end of the string. A quick jerk will make the Yo-Yo bounce back along the floor into your hand.

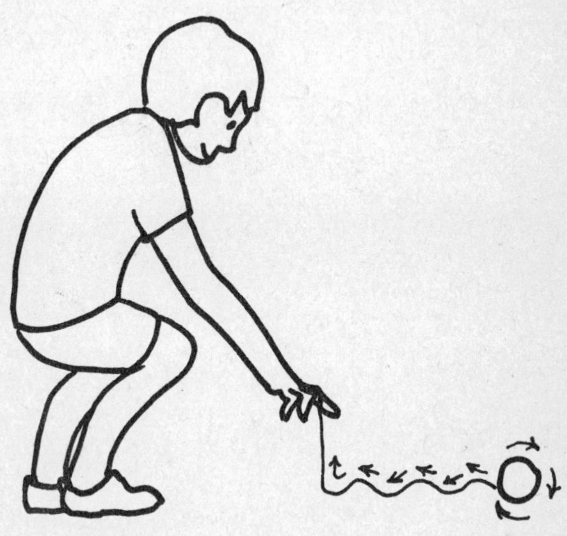

16 THE TUNNEL

This trick is exactly the same as The Creeper, but this time step over the Yo-Yo as it rolls along the floor.

17 THE BUZZ SAW

1 Throw a spinner, but this time lower it onto a crumpled piece of paper. It will make a noise exactly like a buzz saw.

18 SPAGHETTI

1 Throw a spinner.

2 With your left hand grasp the string 5cms/2ins below your right hand, so that it takes the weight of the Yo-Yo.

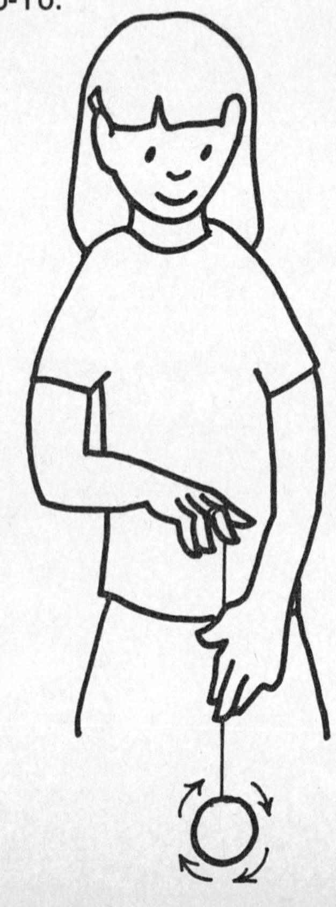

3 Then with your right hand, grasp the string again, beneath the left hand. Repeat this with alternate hands, until you have a handful of looped string looking like spaghetti.

4 Release the string, give a sharp jerk, and the Yo-Yo will return to your hand.

HARDER TRICKS

19 OUT, UP AND DOWN

1 Fling the Yo-Yo straight out in front of you.

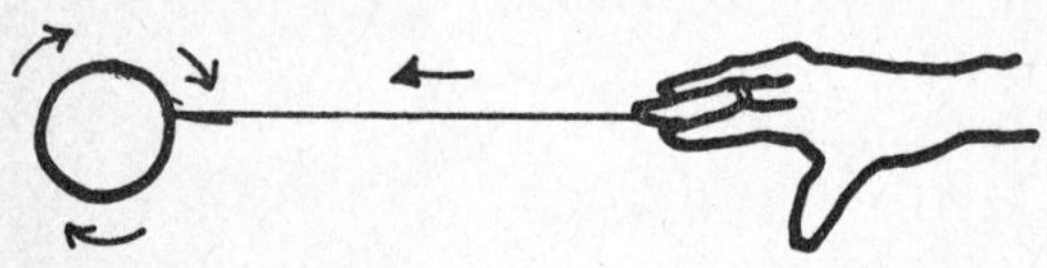

2 Jerk it back rapidly, flick it under your hand (palm facing inwards), and straight up.

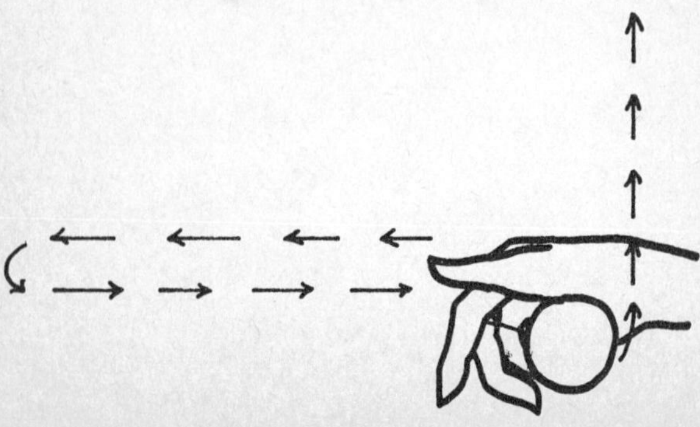

3 Turn your palm up and jerk the Yo-Yo back. Let it fall past your hand. Catch it on its return flight up the string.

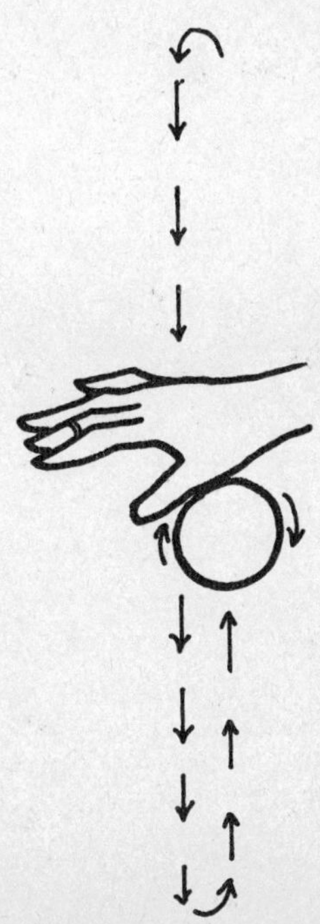

20 UP, OUT AND UP AGAIN

1 Fling the Yo-Yo straight up.

2 Bring your hand down, turning wrist, and fling the Yo-Yo out in front.

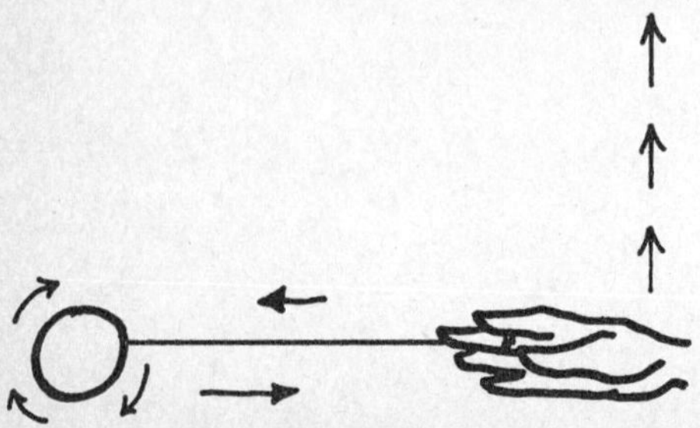

3 Draw back quickly, flick the Yo-Yo under your hand and back up in the air, before catching.

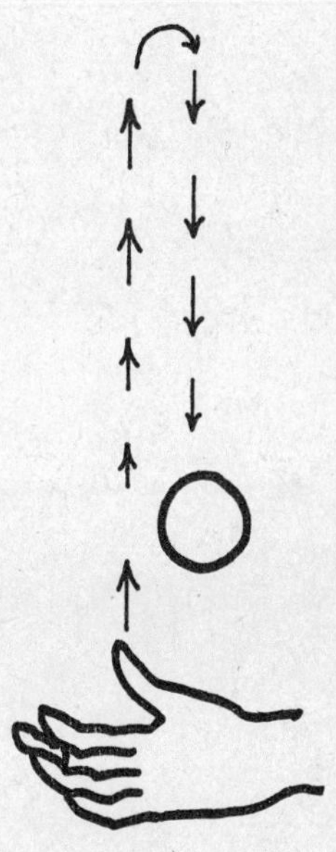

21 PAT THE BABY

1 Throw a spinner.

2 When you want the Yo-Yo to return, smartly hit the back of your hand.

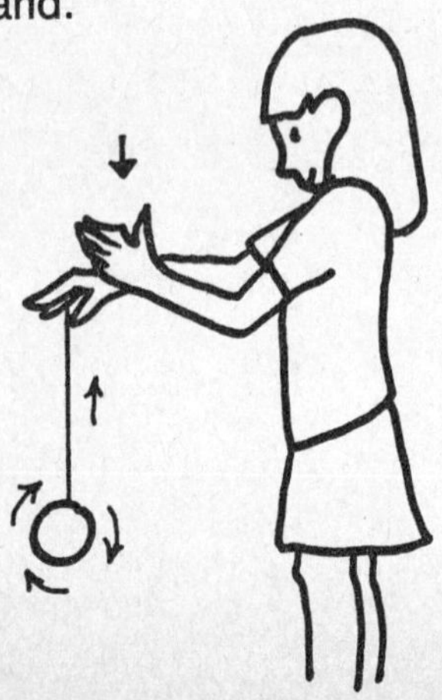

22 THE CATCH

1 Throw an ‘up and down’ Yo-Yo.

2 Before it reaches the bottom of the string, slip the knot off your finger and hold the string just below the loop.

3 When the Yo-Yo is nearly at the top of the string, give a slight jerk and let go. The Yo-Yo will fly into the air, and you can catch it in your hand.

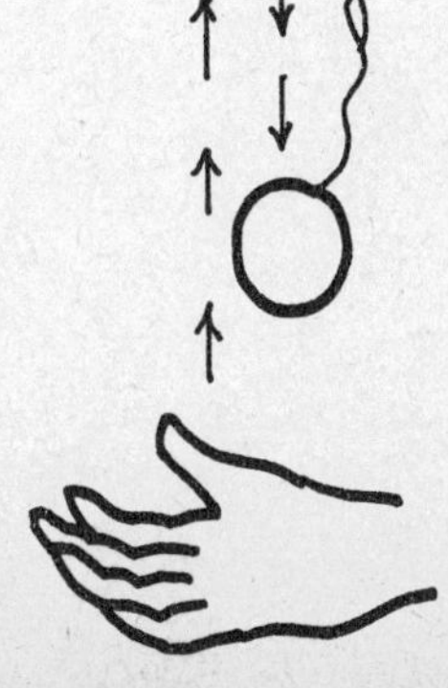

23 SKY ROCKET

1 Throw a fast spinner.

2 Whilst the Yo-Yo is spinning slip the string off your finger.

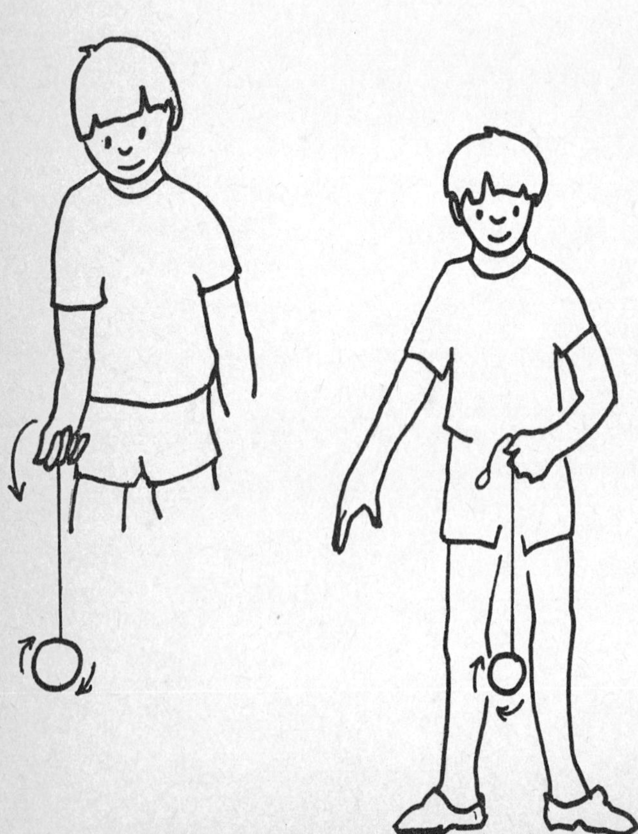

3 Give a strong jerk so that the Yo-Yo starts to climb. Then let go and it will fly high in the air. Try to catch it in your hands, or in a pocket.

24 ROUND THE CORNER

1 Throw a fast spinner.

2 Lift your hand beside your head, letting the string of the Yo-Yo hang behind your elbow.

3 With the string looped over the upper part of your arm, bring your hand down until it is about 8cms/3ins from the Yo-Yo. Grasp the string and give it a quick jerk.

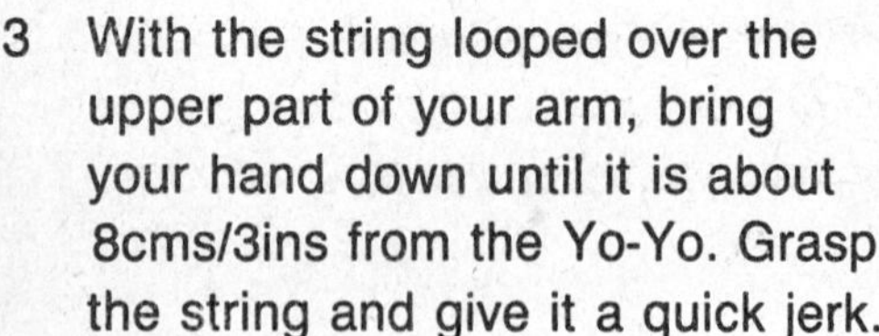

4 This will make the Yo-Yo climb rapidly up the string, over your arm and back down in front of you. It will then return up the string to your hand.

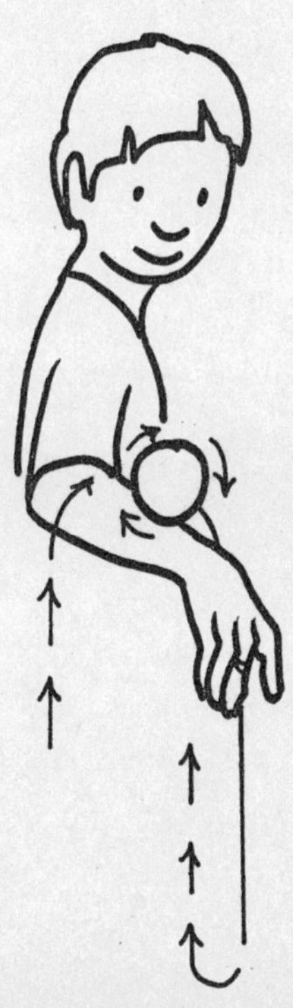

25 OVER THE FALLS

1 Start this trick with your arm swinging at your side, with the palm of your hand facing backwards holding the Yo-Yo.

2 Swing your arm forwards, at the same time releasing the Yo-Yo.

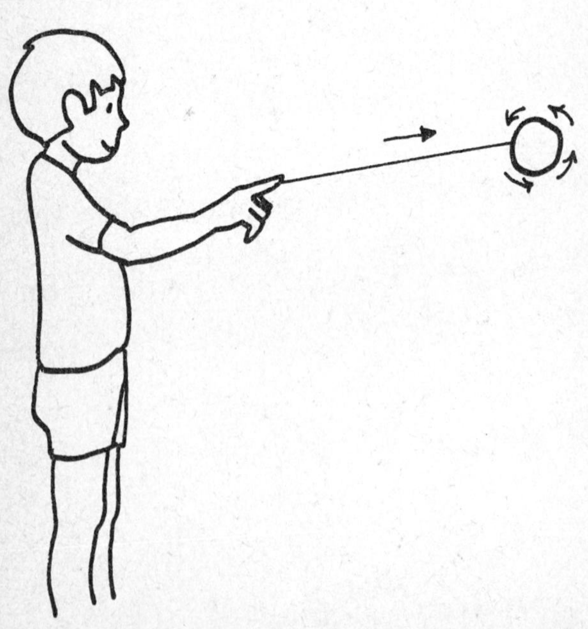

3 As it starts the return flight, curve your wrist upwards, and then allow the Yo-Yo to drop straight down. After it reaches the bottom of the string it will return to your hand.

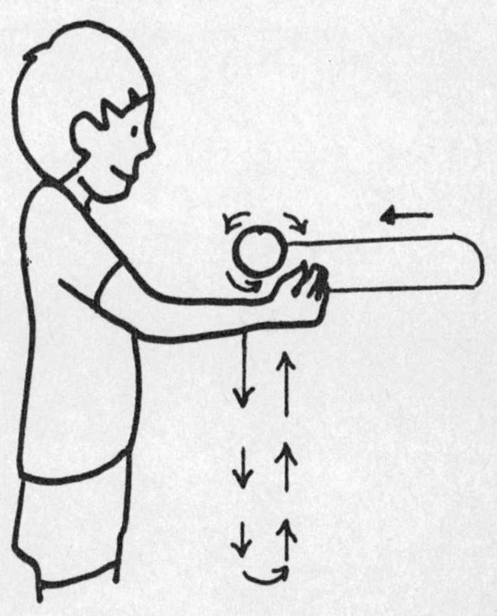

26 AROUND THE WORLD

1 Start the trick with your arm swinging normally at your side. Hold the Yo-Yo in your hand with the palm facing backwards.

2 Snap your arm upwards, releasing the Yo-Yo at the start of this movement. Your arm should continue moving until it is in front of your body at about shoulder height.

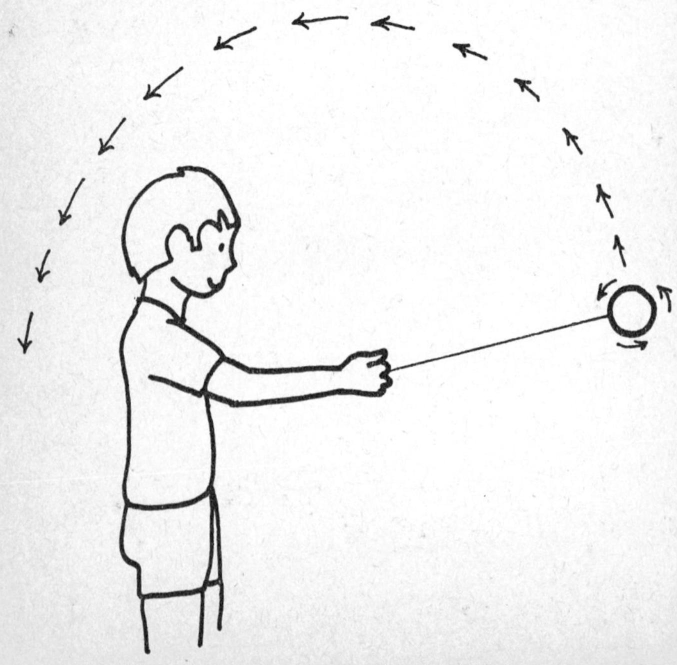

3 The Yo-Yo will be spinning freely at the end of the string, but the impetus will carry the string in a complete circle.

4 After completing the circle, a slight jerk will make the Yo-Yo return to your hand.

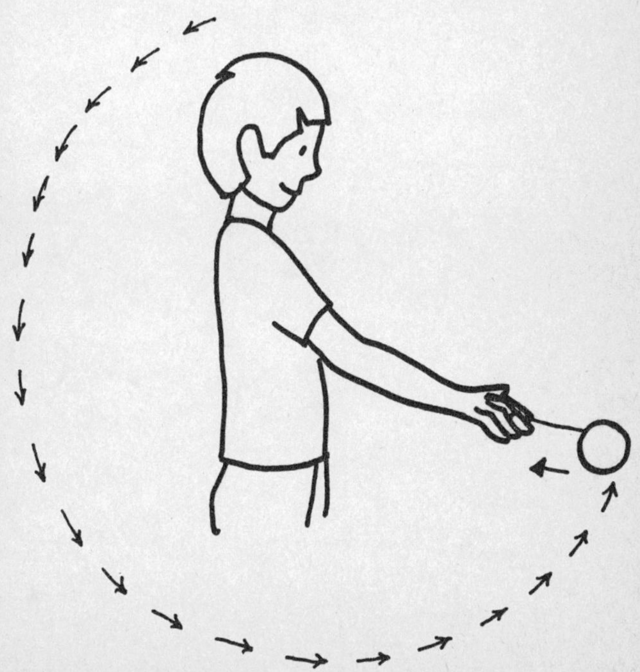

27 THE LIFT

1 Throw a fast spinner.

2 Grasp the string with your left hand, roughly half way between the spinning Yo-Yo and your right hand.

3 Then with your right hand, grasp the string again, about 2½cms/1in from the spinning Yo-Yo.

4 Rapidly slide the excess string through your right hand, so that the Yo-Yo descends. The sudden movement will cause the Yo-Yo to climb up the string and down again.

28 JUMP THE FENCE

1 Throw a normal up-and-down Yo-Yo.

2 On its return flight, instead of catching the Yo-Yo, a quick flick of the wrist will send it over the top of your hand and back down the other side.

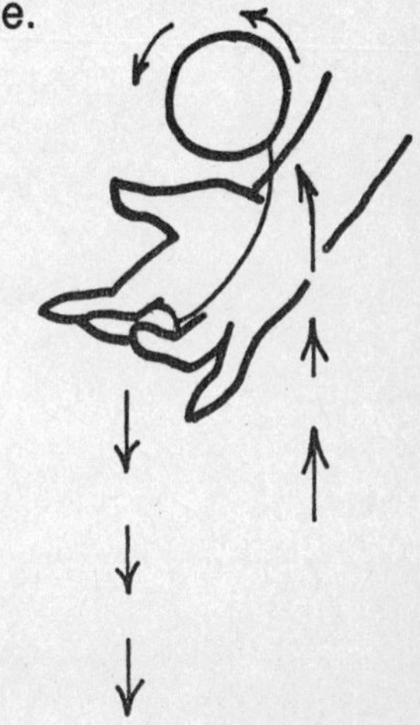

3 Catch it in your hand on the next return flight.

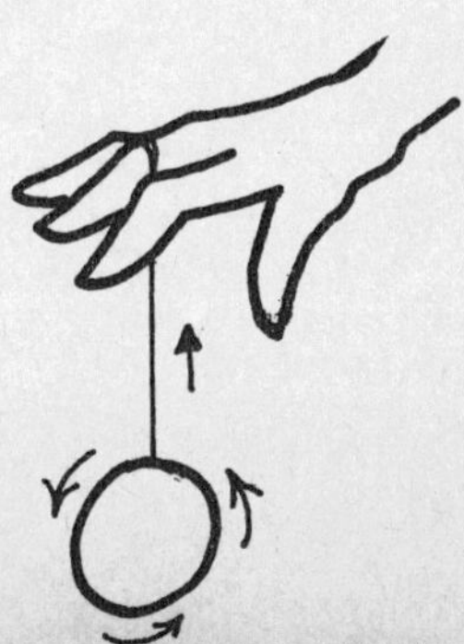

29 ROCK THE BABY

1 Throw a fast spinner.

2 Reach out as far as you can in front of you with your left hand, and grasp the middle of the string.

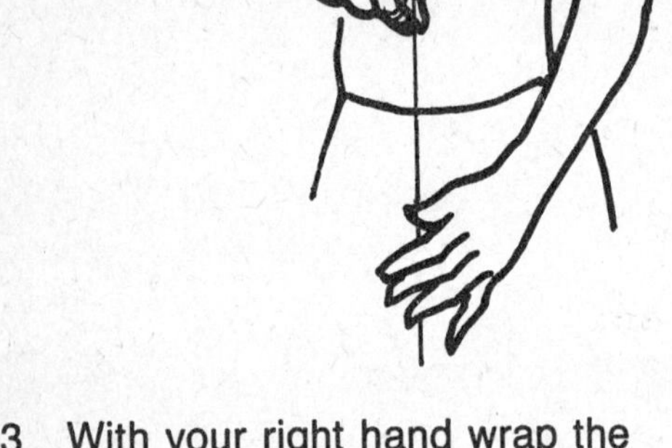

3 With your right hand wrap the string over the knuckles of your left hand, catching the string about 13cms/5ins from the Yo-Yo, so making a large loop.

4 Drop your left hand, with the fingers spread wide apart to make a cradle. Let the Yo-Yo swing backwards and forwards a couple of times. Then drop the Yo-Yo at the same time letting go of the string with your left hand. The Yo-Yo will fall to the end of the string, and return to your hand.

30 THREAD THE NEEDLE

1 Throw a fast spinner.

2 Holding your left hand in front of you, wrap the string over your left forefinger. It will look as if there are two strands of string over this finger.

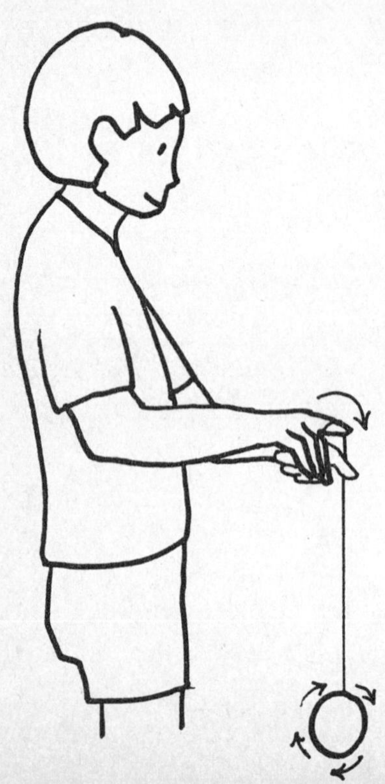

3 Thread one of these strands through the notch which goes round the middle of the Yo-Yo. The Yo-Yo will continue to spin. To return the Yo-Yo slip your left forefinger from the loop, then give a slight jerk to bring it back to your hand.

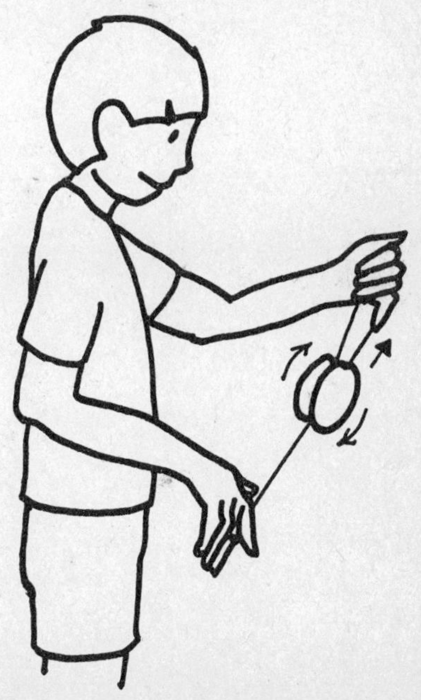

HARDER STILL

31 SKIN THE CAT

1 Throw a spinner down, and backwards.

2 Slide the index finger of your free hand under the string until it is about 10cms/4ins from the spinning Yo-Yo.

3 With a sharp flick of the wrist bring the Yo-Yo up in a circle, over your hand, towards your body and then out in front.

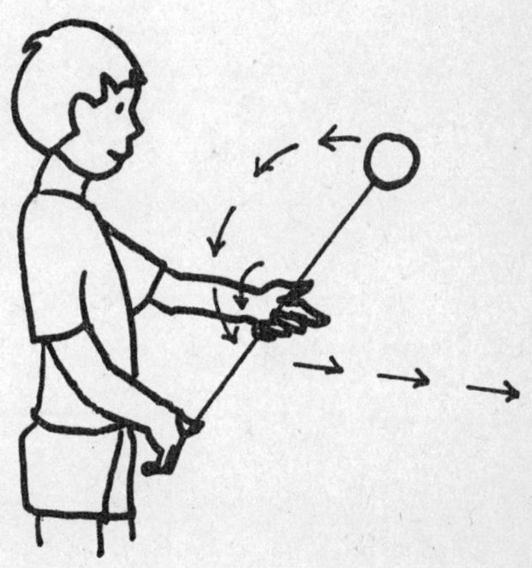

4 The Yo-Yo will then return to your hand.

32 THE FOUNTAIN

1 Start by swinging your arm at your side, palm facing backwards.

2 Throw the Yo-Yo forwards and upwards.

3 As the Yo-Yo starts to fall, curve your wrist in a circular motion and snap the Yo-Yo backwards and upwards.

4 When it reaches its highest point, snap your wrist again sharply in a circular motion, so that the Yo-Yo travels forward. Then let the Yo-Yo return to your hand.

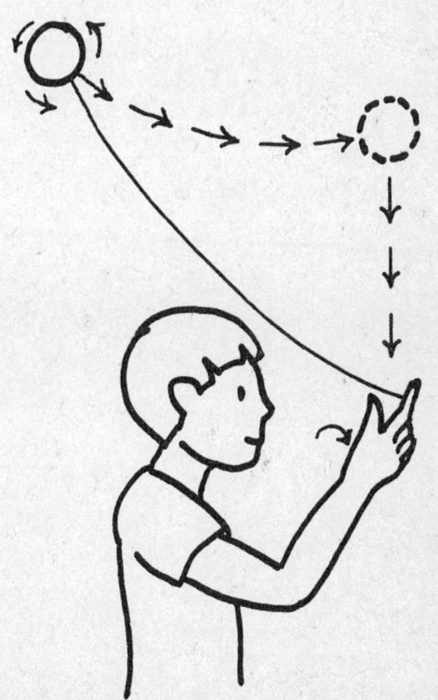

33 THE PENDULUM

1 Throw a spinner out in front of you, just before it reaches shoulder height, give a quick twitch.

2 The Yo-Yo will swing down and up in a semi-circle behind you, also at shoulder height, another twitch will bring it back again

34 THE PENNY FARTHING (a variation on Around the World)

1 Start with your arm swinging normally at your side, with the Yo-Yo in your hand, palm facing backwards.

2 Snap your arm upwards, at the same time releasing the Yo-Yo. Your arm continues moving until it is about shoulder height in front of you.

3 Allow the Yo-Yo to make one complete circuit, but at the last moment a sharp flick of the wrist will allow the Yo-Yo to make a small additional circle around your hand.

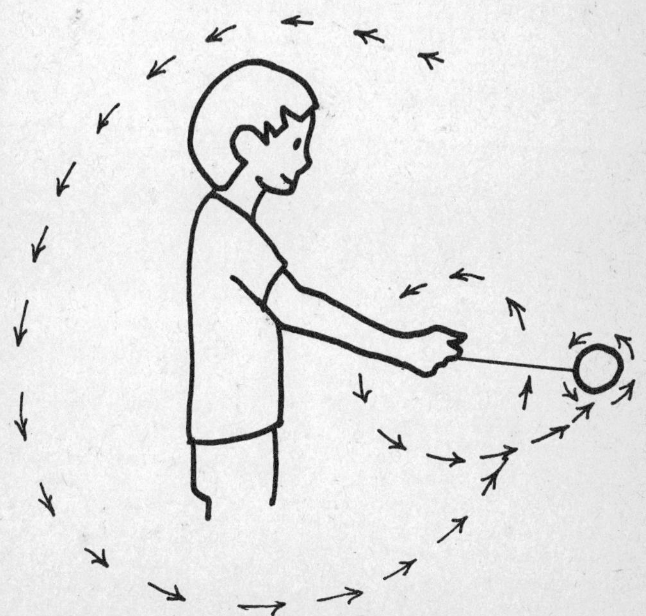

35 LOOP THE LOOP

1 Start with your arm swinging normally at your side.

2 Throw the Yo-Yo out in front of you.

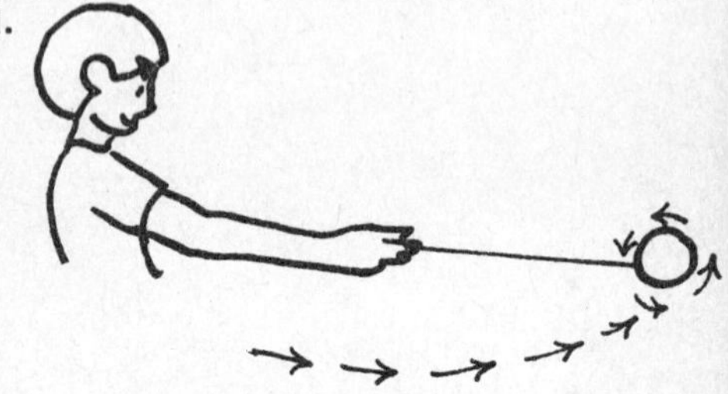

3 On its return flight, instead of catching it, snap your wrist with a circular motion, leaving your hand and arm extended in front of you.

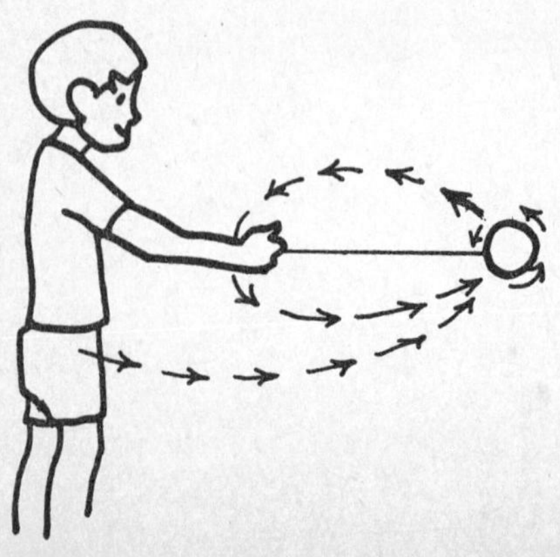

4 The Yo-Yo will go over your hand, and out in front of you again. Repeat stage 3, and see how many loops you can keep going. The record is over 1,000! NOTE: Loops should always go inside your arm.

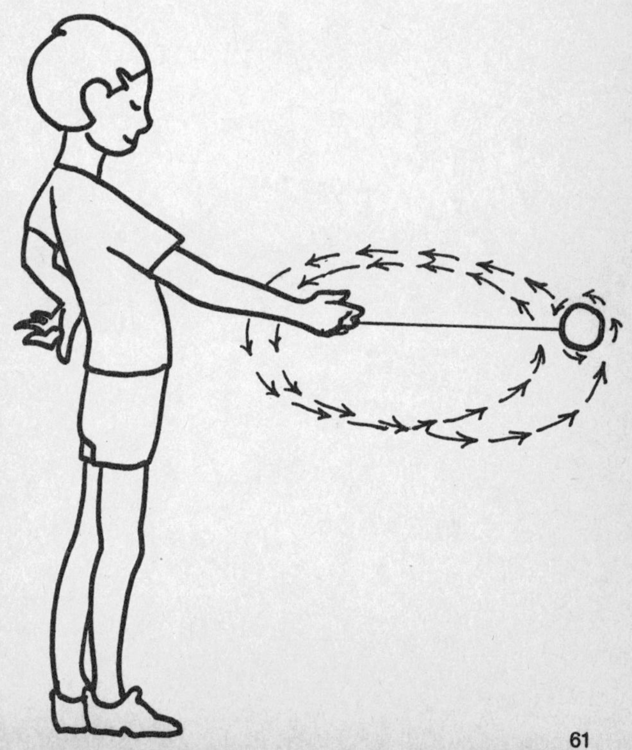

36 THE SPECTACLES

1 Throw a fast spinner in front of you to about head height.

2 Give a sharp twitch, and turn your body. Instead of catching the Yo-Yo, fling it down, so that its impetus carries it up to head height on the other side of your body.

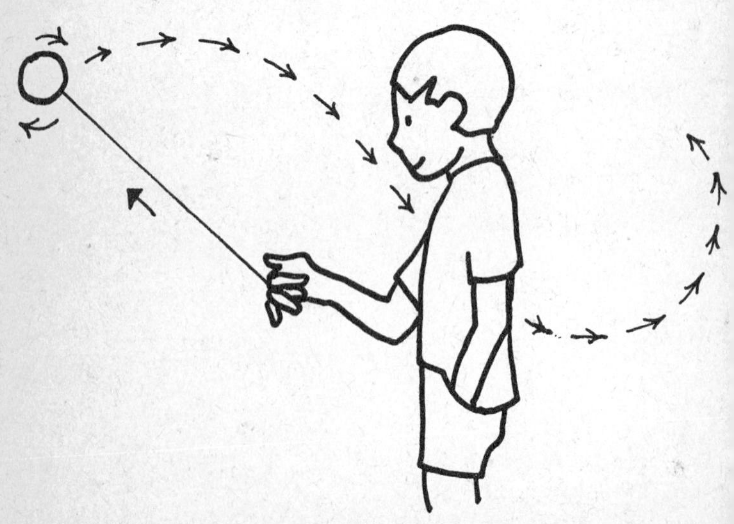

3 Then let it fall back down and return to your hand.

37 DOG BITE (NB: Girls will need to wear trousers to do this trick)

1 Throw a fast spinner between your legs.

2 A quick jerk backwards should allow the groove in the Yo-Yo to catch onto your trousers. But it won't work with skintight jeans!

38 ELEPHANT TRUNK

For this trick you will need a chair.

1 Throw a fast spinner forwards so that the Yo-Yo string loops itself over the back of a chair, where it should continue spinning.

2 If you are very clever, a quick jerk will bring the Yo-Yo back from its position and into your hand.

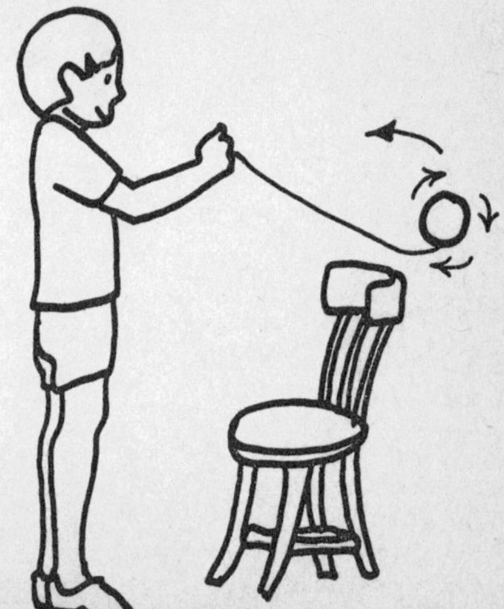

39 PUNCH BAG

1 Throw the Yo-Yo out in front of you.

2 Instead of catching the Yo-Yo on its return, a quick flick of the wrist will bring it back inside and over the top of your hand.

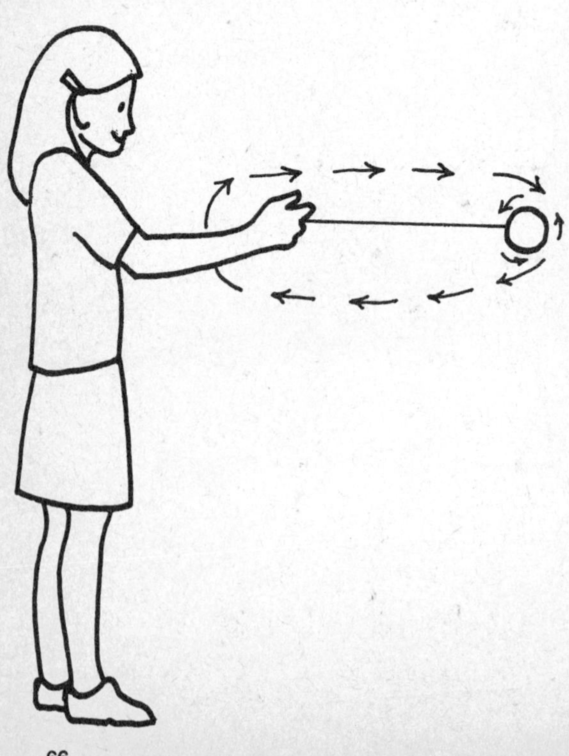

3 And straight out in front again. Catch the Yo-Yo on its return flight.

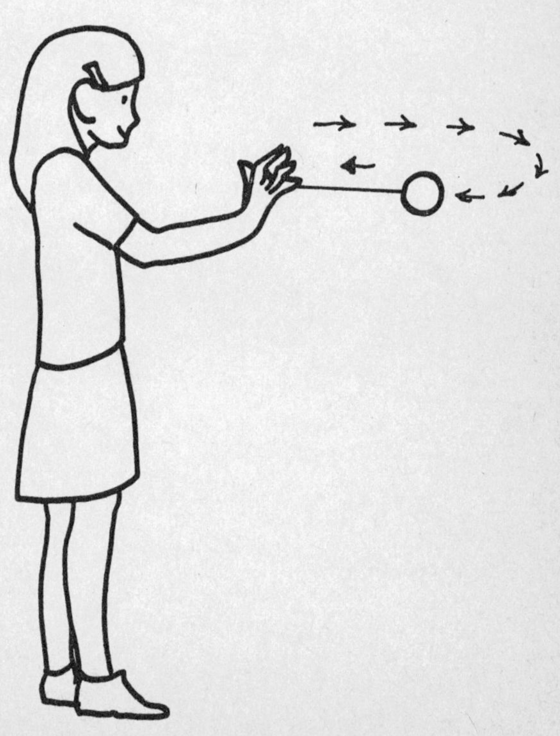

40 BREAKAWAY

1 Bend wrist and arm upwards from elbow at your side.

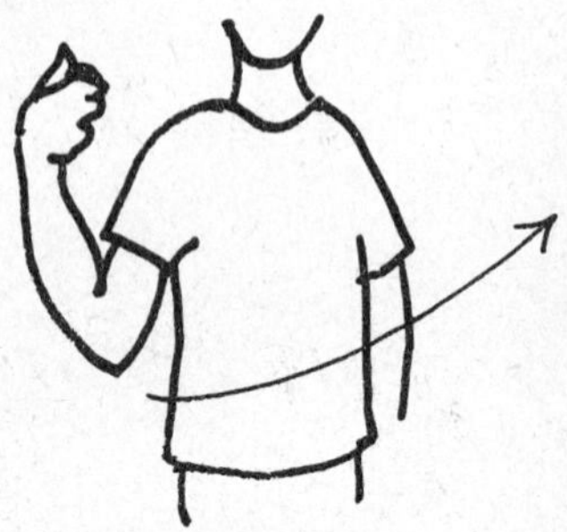

2 Snapping arm down, throw a spinner, outwards and across your body. On reaching the end of the string the Yo-Yo will spin, briefly defying gravity.

3 The Yo-Yo will then fall in a downward curve and return to your hand

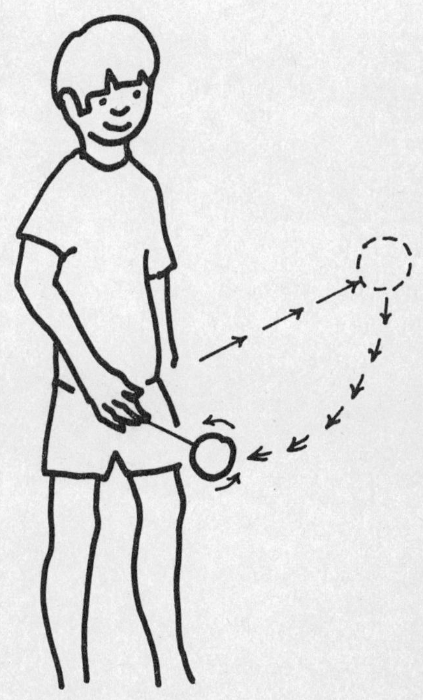

41 WINDMILL

1 Bend wrist and arm upwards from elbow at your side.

2 Snapping the arm down, throw a spinner, outwards and across your body.

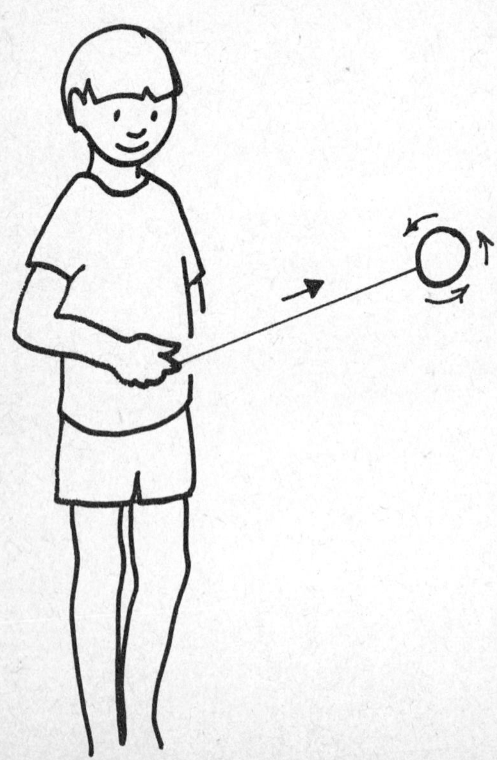

3 With index finger of the left hand, catch the string from above, a little way from the Yo-Yo, so that it will wrap itself around your finger once and then unwind.

4 Catch the Yo-Yo in your right hand.

42 MAN ON A TIGHTROPE

1 Bend wrist and arm upwards from elbow at your side.

2 Snapping the arm down, throw a spinner, outwards and across your body.

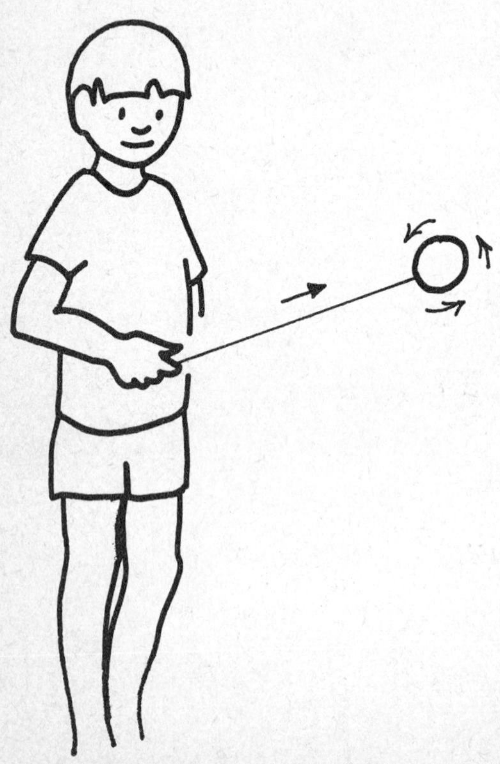

3 With index finger of the left hand, catch the string from above, so that once again the Yo-Yo jumps over your finger: but this time catch the Yo-Yo on its own string, where it will continue to spin.

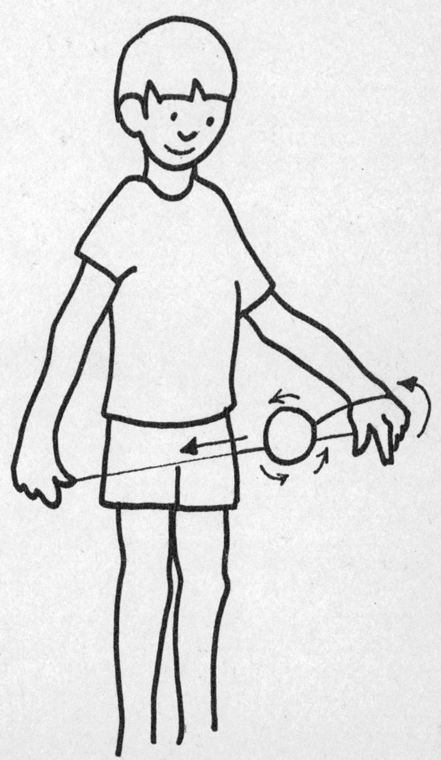

43 FLYING SAUCER

NB: For this trick you need a Yo-Yo with a string wound fairly loosely around its axle.

1 Throw a sideways fast spinner.

2 A rapid shake of your wrist will cause the string to wriggle.

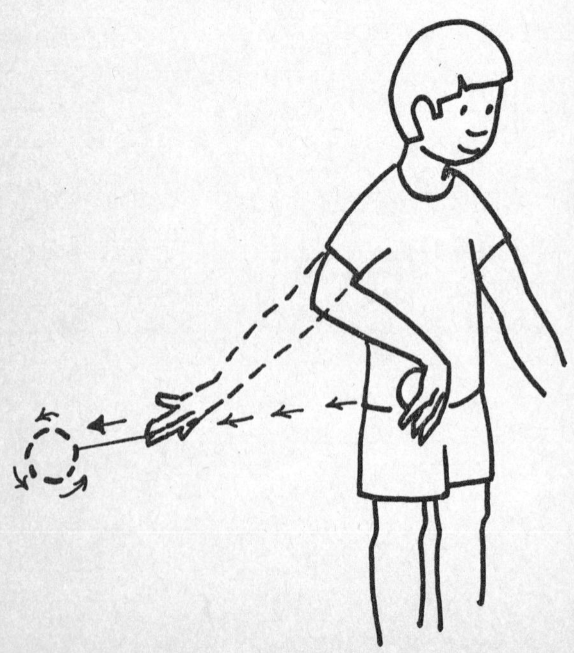

3 Bring your left hand across, and gather up the string with the middle finger of the left hand, so that the Yo-Yo continues to spin on its side.

44 THREE LEAF CLOVER

1 Start with your hand swinging at your side, the Yo-Yo in your hand, palm facing backwards.

2 Throw in an upward swing above your head. As the Yo-Yo comes back, flick your wrist, and send the Yo-Yo out in front of you. (Same movement as Loop the Loop.)

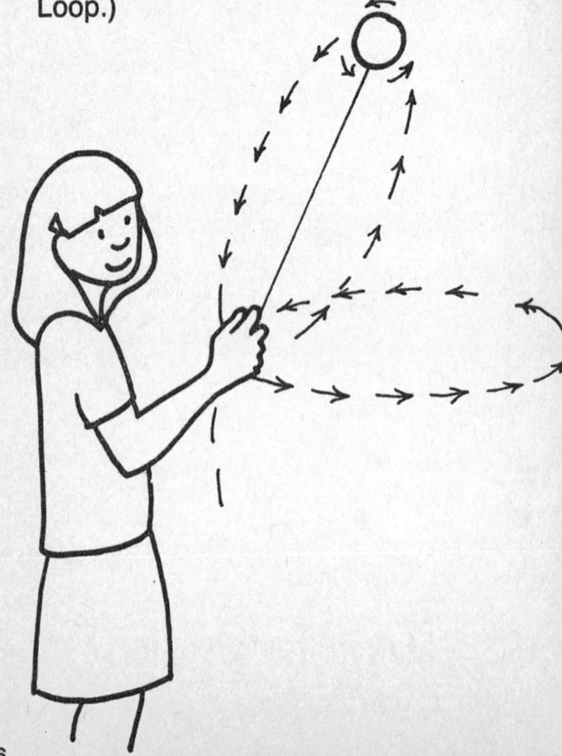

3 When the Yo-Yo returns, flick your wrist again, this time sending the Yo-Yo in a downward motion.

4 Let the Yo-Yo return to your hand as normal.

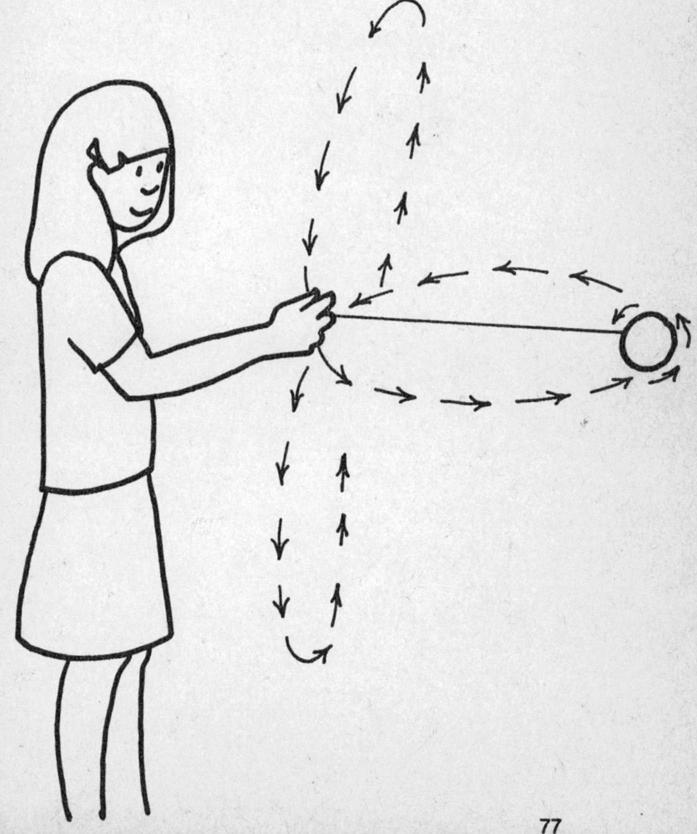

45 REVERSE LOOPS

Virtually the same trick as Loop the Loop but:

1 Start with your hand in front of your body, ready to throw the Yo-Yo backwards.

2 On its return flight, snap the wrist in a circular motion.

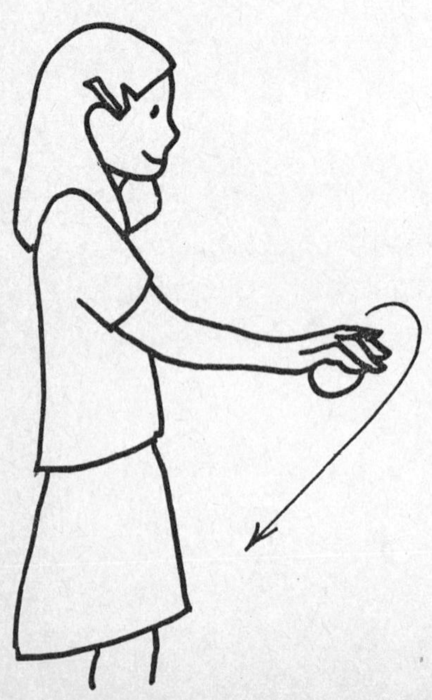

3 The Yo-Yo will go over your hand and back again. Keep the Loops going for as long as possible.

TRICKS WITH TWO YO-YOS

46 TANGO

1 Take a Yo-Yo in each hand and throw two fast spinners.

2 Extend fingers of both hands as wide apart as possible.

3 Bring string of left hand Yo-Yo across until it lies in front and between thumb and index finger of right hand. Hook thumb round string.

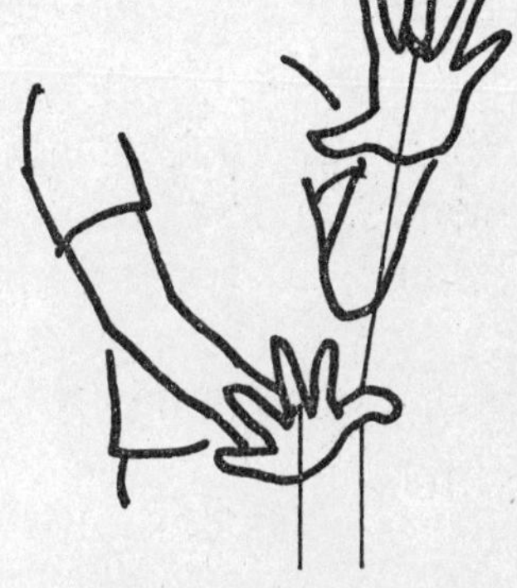

4 Then lower the thumb of left hand and loop it round right hand string in same manner.

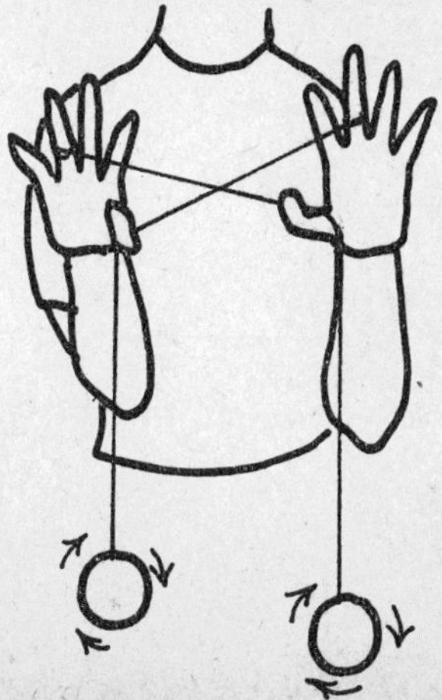

47 DOUBLE HANDED LOOP THE LOOP

1 Take a Yo-Yo in each hand and throw a normal forward Loop the Loop with the right hand.

2 When the right hand Loop the Loop is well under way, throw a second Loop the Loop with the left hand, at the point where the first Loop the Loop is at its furthest position forward.

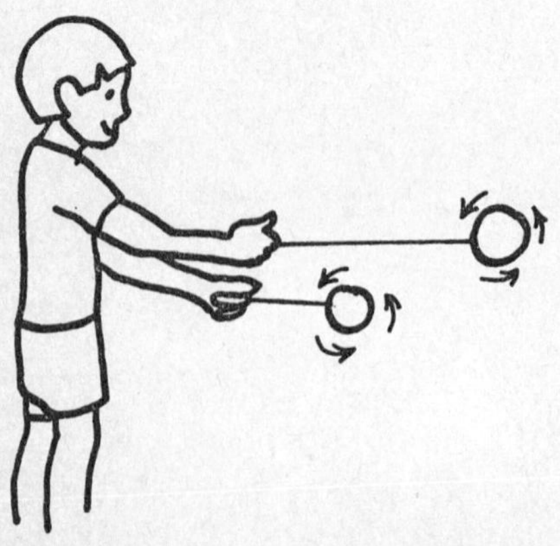

3 This will ensure that one Yo-Yo is going forward as the other is returning to your hand.

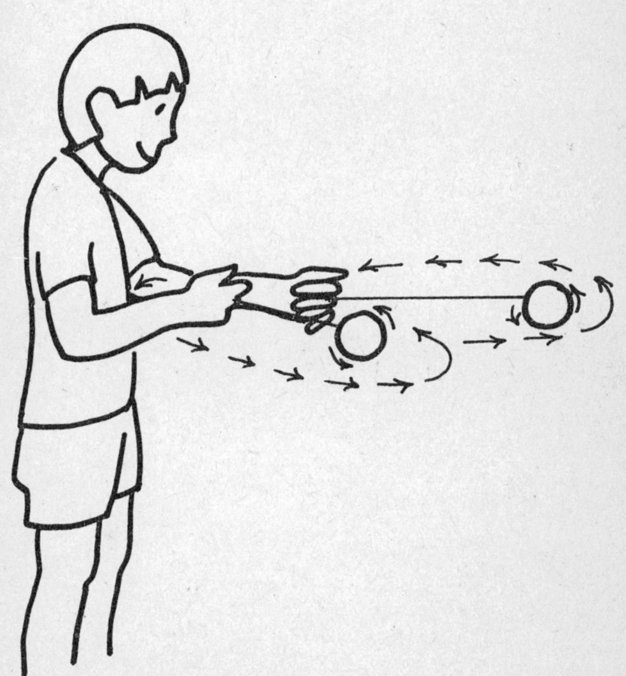

48 FOUNTAIN AND LOOP THE LOOP

1 With right hand, throw the Yo-Yo in a forward and upward movement and continue the Fountain trick as described on page 54.

2 At the same time throw a forward Loop the Loop with your left hand.

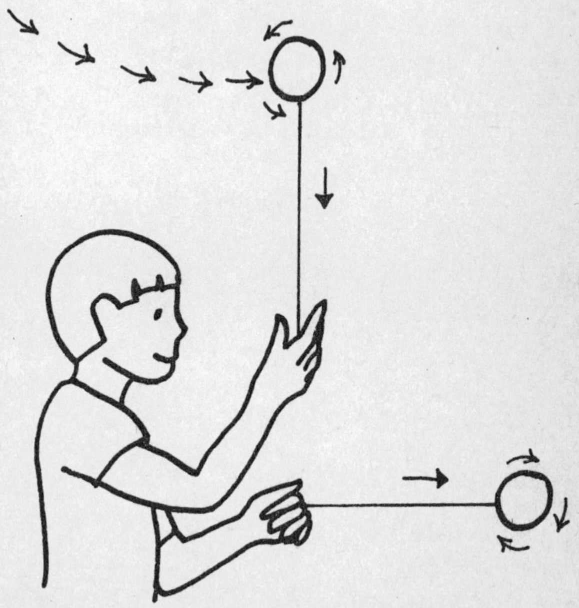

49 DOUBLE FOUNTAIN

This is the hardest trick in the whole book, and considered to be almost impossible, but you can have a lot of fun trying it. It probably helps to be ambidextrous.

There are two ways of approaching this trick. The first is to throw a Fountain with your right hand several times, until it is working smoothly. Then try joining in with the left hand. Alternatively, it is possible to try starting with both hands at the same time.

50 CRISS-CROSS

This is yet another variation on Loop the Loop.

1 As with the double-handed version, you start by throwing a Loop the Loop with your right hand, but instead of sending it straight forward, send it diagonally across the front of your body.

2 Throw the second Loop the Loop, also diagonally across your body, when the first one is on its return flight.

Have fun, and watch out that the strings don't get tangled up!

You can of course try two-handed versions of some of the other tricks such as Walk the Dog, or Over the Falls.

COMPETITION RULES

In most competitions you will be expected to perform the twelve basic tricks listed on the opposite page. Every competitor is allowed two attempts at each of the first eleven tricks. Failure to achieve any trick means elimination from the contest. To complete any trick successfully, the Yo-Yo must end up in the competitor's hand with the string fully wound.

At the end of this first session, all competitors who have successfully completed the eleven tricks have to try to keep the Loop the Loop trick going for as long as possible. The person who can perform most consecutive Loop the Loops is declared the winner.

The tricks are:

1 Up and Down (see page 10).
2 Throws: Down, Out and Up (see pages 16/17).
3 The Spinner, including return to hand (see pages 18/19).
4 Walking the Dog (see pages 22/23).
5 Creeper (see pages 24/25).
6 Round the corner (see pages 38/39).
7 Skin the Cat (see pages 52/53).
8 Rock the Baby (see pages 48/49).
9 Spaghetti (see pages 28/29).
10 The Lift (see pages 44/45).
11 Thread the Needle (see pages 50/51).
12 Loop the Loop (see pages 60/61).

HISTORY OF THE YO-YO

The first Yo-Yo was a primitive weapon used in the Philippines. A thong was tied round a piece of stone and hurled at the unsuspecting quarry!

The Yo-Yo next appeared in Ancient Greece where it was called Disc.

It resurfaced in Britain in the 18th century under the name of 'Bandalore' or 'Quiz'. It was very popular.

Next the craze swept through France. Some aristocrats were even playing with Yo-Yos as they mounted the steps to the Guillotine!

In the 1920s the 'Yo-Yo' first got its name. It was registered by Mr Duncan of the USA. Duncan Yo-Yos have been made ever since.

The first ever World Yo-Yo Championship was held in London in 1932.

The Philippinos still play with Yo-Yos carved from wood, bone and horn. The word Yo-Yo is said to mean "come back" in Philippino.

INDEX